WoEB

What on Earth Books is an imprint of What on Earth Publishing
Allington Castle, Maidstone, Kent ME16 0NB, United Kingdom
30 Ridge Road Unit B, Greenbelt, Maryland, 20770, United States

First published in the United Kingdom in 2022

Written by John Francis
Illustrated by Josy Bloggs

Index by DataWorks
Print and Production Consultancy Booklabs.co.uk

Staff for this book: Nancy Feresten, Publisher; Laura Buller, Editorial Director; Katy Lennon, Senior Editor; Andy Forshaw, Art Director; Daisy Symes, Designer.

With special thanks to: Catherine Brereton, Dr. María Dolores Cervera (Cinvestav-Mexico), Joshua Coombes, Satu Fox, Roshi Joan Halifax, Michelle Harris, Priyanka Lamichhane, Sophie Macintyre, Liane Onish, Jon W. Parmenter, Brad Powless and Adrianne Velasco.

A CIP catalogue record for this book is available from the British Library

Published and Distributed in India by Scholastic India Pvt. Ltd.

ISBN: 978-93-5954-063-4

This reprint edition : January, 2025

Printed in India : VK Global Digital Private Limited

Human Kindness

Words of thanks from the author

I first would like to thank my wife Martha and my sons Sam and Luke for maintaining a home spirit where I could practise and write on kindness. With them, I have mostly been on the receiving side. I also want to thank my friend Chris Lloyd who asked if I would write about kindness. His request reinforced a meditation practice on kindness and gratitude. Thank you to the librarians at the University of Wisconsin who sent much-needed articles and books to help my research. And I would be remiss if I did not thank my editors, Katy Lennon and Catherine Brereton, and the whole What on Earth staff, who supported me in this endeavour.

I would like to dedicate this book to Planetwalkers everywhere and to all of our teachers.

Human Kindness

True Stories of Compassion and Generosity that Changed the World

By John 'The Planetwalker' Francis
Illustrated by Josy Bloggs

What on Earth Books

Contents

Foreword

So many times, I have heard His Holiness the Dalai Lama say: 'My religion is kindness.' This simple but powerful statement is at the very heart of *Human Kindness* by environmentalist and deep friend of the Earth, John Francis – the book that you are reading.

John Francis is a truly remarkable human being, who for 17 years, walked in silence and solidarity with our planet. He walked as a living example of non-violence toward our Earth and its inhabitants. And he was the recipient of great kindness along the way. By his very presence, he embodied kindness and gave kindness to those whom he met on his long and dedicated walk.

From this experience of pilgrimage, John discovered the profound value of caring and compassion and its immeasurable benefits for those who receive it, those who give it and those who witness it. Throughout his courageous life, John has watered the seeds of kindness and compassion in thousands of others, too.

Kindness and compassion come in many different sizes and shapes: a rescue or a smile; food for the hungry or a caring hand; or a project, like Upaya's Nomads Clinic. I began the Nomads Clinic project in 1981 in response to the suffering I witnessed in the far reaches of Nepal, where medical care was not accessible. Our aim was to bring health care to people in remote villages and nomad's camps in the high Himalayas. This project continues even today, thanks to our Nepali medical colleagues.

Like the Nomads Clinic, there have been so many beautiful ripple effects from John's long pilgrimage of kindness. This book is one of the gifts of his dedication. At the end of his many years of silence, he has become a voice for the Earth and all species, and this precious book reminds us that we can meet this world with kindness, too.

Roshi Joan Halifax
Abbot
Upaya Zen Center

Introduction

Kindness comes in many forms. Sometimes it's a big gesture like saving someone from a burning building. Other times it might be as small and simple as a smile. Kindness includes generosity, which means sharing what you have with others without expecting anything in return. And it also includes compassion. When someone is compassionate, they try to understand other people's feelings and troubles. Compassion also means treating other living things on our planet, such as plants and animals, with respect.

In this book you will find many examples of kindness. Some kind acts changed the world. Others just brightened someone's day. By looking at these acts of kindness, big and small, we can see how important our own daily acts of kindness can be to our lives and to our world. I hope that in this book you will find stories that inspire and speak to you.

John Francis

My Journey of Kindness

All my life I have been lucky enough to experience kindness in many different ways. This was especially true during the 17 years that I took a vow of silence. During this time I travelled by foot and met many amazing people. Here are just a few moments of kindness and compassion that led me to writing this book for you.

1946 onwards

My parents taught me to look after the squirrels and birds that lived around our home. They also taught me to be kind to people and expect kindness in return.

1976

On another walk in Oregon, a kind family fed me when I had no food. In return I stayed to help them build a new house. I learned that kindness creates kindness: because the family helped me, I wanted to help them too.

1975

I walked to southern Oregon, USA, and two gold miners gave me shelter and dinner in their log cabin. They told me that for them, it was not gold that had the greatest value. Instead, living in nature and treating each other with kindness were most important to them.

1984

I walked for two years to get to the University of Montana. I had no money for tuition, so the director gave me money to register for environmental studies classes. In 1987, I received a similar kindness at the University of Wisconsin. There, my tuition and living costs were paid for as I studied. I will be forever grateful for these incredible gestures.

1987

I headed east across America. I stopped at the Cheyenne River Sioux Tribe Reservation in Eagle Butte, South Dakota. The local people kindly fed me and gave me a place to rest. Each day someone from the tribe walked with me to keep me company.

1950s

My mother and her friend took gift baskets of fruit and sweets to residents of care homes. I would go with them to be part of their act of kindness.

Around 1952

While travelling on a bus to visit family in the American South, I felt sad because Black people like me had to sit at the back of the bus. A woman saw I was upset and gave me a sweet to cheer me up.

1971

I witnessed two oil tankers collide in the San Francisco Bay. The sight of oil polluting the water and harming the wildlife there changed my life forever.

1972

I chose to stop using oil and started a journey walking across America. Soon, I become known as the Planetwalker.

1973

I decided to stop speaking. I continued my Planetwalker journey in silence.

1990

After 17 years spent walking across America, listening to others and studying the environment, I realized that I had something to say. So I started speaking again. I chose the twentieth anniversary of Earth Day – April 22, 1990 – to break my silence. This was to remind myself to always speak up for the environment and other people.

2008

I was invited to speak at the TED conference in California. I spoke about my journey of silence and learning. By doing this, I hoped to spread my message of respect for our planet.

Today

I now live in New Jersey with my own family. We look after each other and the wildlife around us. We care for any birds that fall from trees or baby bunnies when their burrows are flooded by spring rains. I try to teach my children, as my parents taught me, to spread kindness by example.

What is Kindness?

The Earliest Acts of Kindness

Kindness may be as old as humanity itself. It is difficult to know exactly how people lived in prehistoric times because there are no written records. However, archaeologists have studied the bones of our ancestors to find clues. They have found that prehistoric humans may have showed kindness to one another. This was likely shown by caring for others in their community.

Caring cave dwellers

In 1957, an archaeologist found a skeleton that was 45,000 years old. It is one of the earliest pieces of evidence for kindness by a close human relative. The skeleton was found in Iraq and was named 'Shanidar 1'. The skeleton shows that Shanidar 1 suffered many injuries, some of which left him with a damaged skull and arm. It is possible that he had sight and hearing loss, too. Despite these injuries, he lived into his 40s. That was very old for humans at that time! This means he was probably cared for by friends or family members. They may have taken care of his wounds and helped him find food and shelter.

Ancient Ideas of Kindness

Humans first began to write things down around the year 3,400 BCE. Ancient texts help historians work out what life was like long ago. We can find out about the beliefs that people in the past lived by from what they chose to write down. We can also learn what they thought was important. Life was tough in the ancient world. Many wars were fought over resources such as land and water. However, there were many people who chose peace and kindness.

Human society has changed a lot. Yet many of our beliefs are still influenced by ancient thinkers. Here are some lessons about kindness and compassion from long ago.

Ancient Roman thoughts

Marcus Aurelius was the Emperor of Rome between 161–180 CE. In his book *Meditations*, he wrote about kindness. He suggested that people should choose to be kind even if others are unkind to them.

Haudenosaunee community

The Haudenosaunee have lived in North America for more than 4,000 years. Since ancient times, they have always made decisions as a community. This tradition continues today. The Haudenosaunee people have great respect for nature and treat the Earth with kindness.

Mesoamerican respect

There are almost no records to tell us what the people of the Mayan Empire (250–900 CE) thought about kindness. However, present Maya practices can give us some clues. The Maya believe that everyone has the ability to be kind. They expect people to help each other, share what they have and respect one another.

Southern African compassion

Many ancient southern African cultures lived by the principle of *ubuntu*. This concept means 'I am because you are'. It reminds us that we are connected to all the people around us. Passed down through the generations, *ubuntu* is still recognized today.

Ancient Greek theatre

The ancient Greek play *The Grouch* was first performed in the year 316 BCE. It contains the first known examples of 'paying it forward'. This is when a person is kind to someone, who then is kind to someone else.

Islamic lessons

The Prophet Muhammad founded the religion of Islam. His actions offer lessons about kindness. In one story from around 600 CE, the Prophet Muhammad saw a person crying as they worked. The person was sick and struggling to grind up grain on a stone mill. So the Prophet took over. He ground the grain so that the worker could rest.

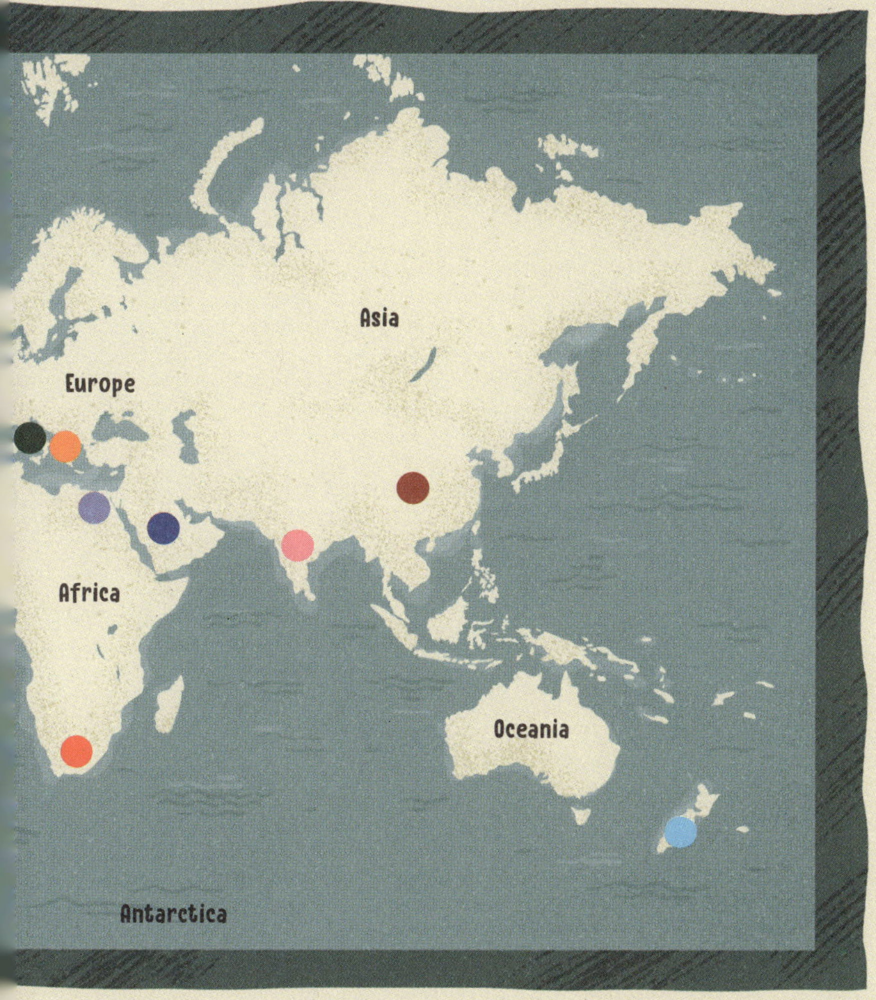

Ancient Chinese society

Confucius was an ancient Chinese scholar. He lived between 551–479 BCE. He believed that a good society was one where everyone was kind to others. He advised kings that they should respect the people they ruled, rather than use their royal power for their own gain.

Ancient Indian peace

The Kalinga War that happened around 260 BCE was fierce. Indian emperor Ashoka the Great saw such terrible bloodshed that he swore never to use violence again. He became known for his kindness, compassion and mercy. He founded hospitals and dug wells to give people access to clean drinking water. He also outlawed cruelty to animals.

Ancient Egyptian writing

In ancient Egypt, one's *ka* was believed to be part of their spirit or soul. Egyptians thought their *ka* encouraged kindness. In their system of picture writing, called hieroglyphics, *ka* was shown by a pair of arms bent upwards at the elbow.

Māori welcome

The Māori settled in what is now New Zealand by about 1200 CE. One of their principles is *manaakitanga*. It means extending love and compassion to others. It is about welcoming visitors and treating people and the environment with love and respect. A traditional Māori greeting is to press one's forehead to the forehead of the guest.

The Golden Rule

From ancient times up to now, people have been thinking of new ways to show kindness. Incredibly, many religions and cultures have come up with a very similar idea. It is called the golden rule. Each version has the same message at its core: treat other people as kindly as you would like to be treated. The rule encourages you to feel empathy. This is when you understand or share someone else's feelings. The rule also helps people know how to act. For example, it tells you not to steal from others, because you wouldn't like if someone stole from you! Here are just a few examples of the many versions of this rule:

'Regard your neighbour's gain as your own gain, and your neighbour's loss as your own loss.'
From *Treatise of the Exalted One on Response and Retribution*, an important Taoist scripture by T'ai Shang Kan Ying P'ien

'I will act towards others exactly as I would act towards myself.'
From the *Siglovada-sutta*, a text that sets out the rules that Buddhists should follow

'Each one should do unto others as they would have others do unto them.'
Manco Cápac, Legendary founder of the Incan empire

'Love your neighbour as yourself.'
From Leviticus 19:18 in the Torah. This is the first part of the Hebrew Bible, which is also known as The Old Testament and is sacred to people of the Jewish and Christian faiths.

'Do not do unto others what you would not want others to do unto you!'
From *The Analects of Confucius*

'As you regard yourself, regard others as well.'
From the *Guru Granth Sahib*, the religious scriptures of Sikhism

'None of you truly believes, until he loves for his brothers what he loves for himself.'
A saying of the Prophet Muhammad, the founder of Islam

'Do not do to another what you do not like to be done to yourself.'
From the *Mahabharata*, an important text in Hinduism

'One going to take a pointed stick to pinch a baby bird should first try it on themself to feel how it hurts.'
Yoruba proverb (Nigeria)

'What you would not find acceptable if it were done to you by another, do not do to them.'
Akan proverb (Ghana)

The Science of Kindness

Humans are social creatures who evolved to live in groups. Being kind is what we do naturally to get along. We tend to be kind to those we love and also others in our community. Studies show that friendliness is one of the reasons why our species has been so successful. Our ancestors worked together to survive challenging times like the freezing cold Ice Age. Being kind also has benefits for us today. It helps our community, is good for our health and can make us happy, too!

Happy hormones

Being kind to others makes us feel good! Good feelings come when our bodies release certain chemicals, called hormones. These chemicals are the body's messengers. Hormones travel in the bloodstream and control many of the body's processes, such as growth and mood. One of the hormones that is released when we are kind is called serotonin. Serotonin makes us feel happy. Another group of hormones are called endorphins. Endorphins relieve stress and pain. Studies show that being kind can reduce blood pressure and improve our immune system so that we can fight off diseases better!

One good turn deserves another

We feel happy when we are kind to others. We also feel happy when someone is kind to us. We even feel happy if we see someone else being kind! Experiencing kindness in any way can lift our spirits. One kind act often inspires another, then another, and on the chain goes.

Is kindness always selfless?

Scientists have spent hundreds of years studying why humans behave the way we do. Deep down, are we selfish creatures who only do good when we benefit from it? Or are we just kind to be kind? Doing something for its own sake, without personal reward is called altruism. But not every act of kindness is altruistic. Sometimes we might be kind so that we feel good about ourselves. Some scientists think that we act kindly because it improves our own health and well-being. Kindness can even help with physical pain. Well, we are only human, and chasing our own happiness is not always a bad thing. If it means we are kind and compassionate to others, then that's awesome!

Stories of Kindness from Around the World

Extreme Bravery

Many stories of kindness feature incredible people who put themselves at risk to save others. Firefighters and other emergency service workers risk their lives to help others every day. But ordinary people do, too. They might need to act in unexpected, and sometimes dangerous, situations in order to help others.

Education for all

Malala Yousafzai was born in the Swat Valley in Pakistan in 1997. In 2008, a group called the Taliban took over the valley and banned girls from going to school. Yousafzai spoke out publicly about how girls have the right to an education. This was a very dangerous thing to do. But Yousafzai put the needs of her community ahead of her own safety. One day, when Yousafzai was 15 years old, a member of the Taliban shot her. She was rushed to hospital for treatment. Thankfully, she made a full recovery and went on to start the Malala Fund. This charity is dedicated to giving all girls the chance to have an education.

Shipwreck survivors

In 1912, the huge British passenger ship RMS *Titanic* sank after hitting an iceberg in the North Atlantic Ocean. Many of the crew and passengers escaped on lifeboats. But there was not enough space for everyone. Sadly, hundreds died. Junior officer Harold Lowe took one boat of passengers to safety, and then returned to look for more survivors. Other senior crew refused. They thought that the people in the water might overload the boats, sinking them all to their deaths. Lowe risked his own life to return to the ice-cold water around the sunken ship. He was able to pull four more people to safety.

Journey to freedom

In the early 1800s there were more than a million enslaved people in the Southern United States. Harriet Tubman was one such person. In 1849, Tubman escaped to freedom. She used the Underground Railroad, a secret network of people and hiding places known as 'stations', that guided people to freedom in the North. After making it to freedom herself, Tubman returned to the South many times. This was incredibly brave. Enslaved people who escaped risked being recaptured, beaten and even killed. Tubman helped around 70 people escape to freedom.

Helping to Heal

Millions of people around the world work in healthcare. These people spend their days helping others. They soothe pain, treat injuries and prevent future sickness. And they will often go to great lengths to help others. The Covid-19 pandemic made many people realize just how important these amazing healthcare professionals are. Here are just a few of the incredible things that they have done.

Sanitation revelation

In 1854, nurse Florence Nightingale went to a hospital in Turkey to care for soldiers during the Crimean War. The wards were dirty and cramped. Sadly, the soldiers often died. But Nightingale noticed that they were dying because of infections and diseases they picked up in hospital, instead of from their wounds. Nightingale worked hard to make the hospital a cleaner, safer place. This helped to save many lives. After returning to England, Nightingale campaigned for cleaner hospitals. She also set up a training school for nurses, which helped lay the foundation for modern standards of cleanliness.

Vaccine volunteers

Viruses have been a threat to humans for thousands of years. Thankfully, we have vaccines to fight them, but they are not always easy to develop. Often we also need brave volunteers to test them. Since the start of the Covid-19 pandemic in 2020, around half a million people in the UK alone have volunteered to take part in vaccine trials. These incredible people put themselves at risk in order to help protect us all.

Mountaineering medics

Everyone will need medical care at some point in their lives. But what if there is no doctor nearby? Many communities live in remote areas with limited, or no access to healthcare. These people often rely on medical teams who are willing to brave extreme conditions to reach them. One such group of intrepid medics is the Nomads Clinic. This group was set up in 1981 by Buddhist teacher Joan Halifax. The project is now organized by Halifax at the Upaya Zen Center in New Mexico, USA. Every year, medics, climbers, support staff and horses set off on a round trip, that is about 274 kilometres long, through the Himalayan mountains in Asia. They bring medicine and offer medical care to the people living there.

Champions of Charity

Another way that people can be kind is through raising money for charity. There are thousands of charities all over the world, each with a different mission. But most have kindness, compassion and generosity at their core. My own charity, called Planetwalk, sponsors people to go on walks. These walks promote environmental education, responsibility and peace. These causes are some of the things that are most important to me. If you were to create a charity, what would you like it to do?

Animal assistance

It's not just people who can benefit from charity – animals can, too! One animal charity is The World Wildlife Fund (WWF). It was founded in 1961 to protect animals that were being threatened by human activities. In its first year, the WWF helped to save animals such as the bald eagle in North America. They also established a small nature reserve in Colombia, South America. Now the WWF is one of the world's most well-known animal charities. One project is providing funding to study and save endangered tigers in Asia. In 2016, the WWF announced that the number of wild tigers had increased for the first time in more than 100 years!

Access to education

Safeena Husain was a young girl who grew up in poverty in New Delhi, India. She managed to leave behind her tough childhood to study at the London School of Economics, and grew up to be a successful adult. But she never forgot where she had come from, and eventually she went back to India to start a charity that helps girls just like her. Now her organization, Educate Girls, is working to help millions of girls go to school so they can also follow their dreams.

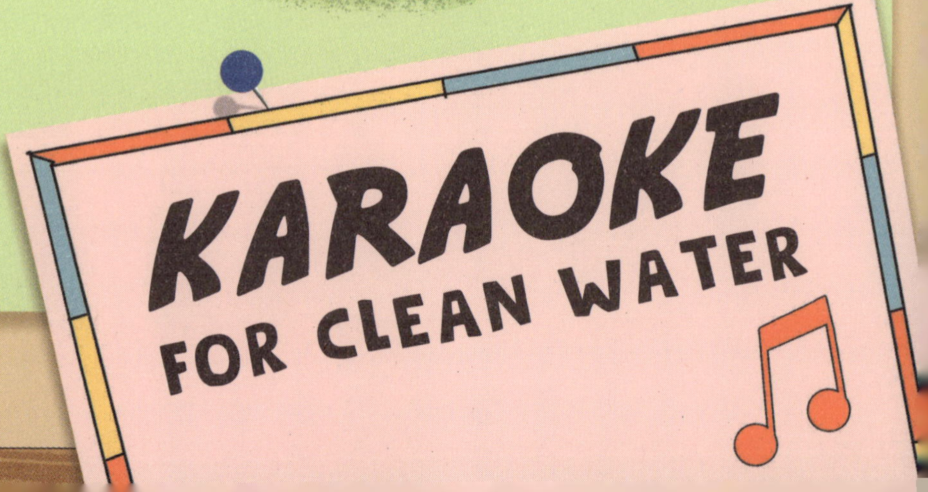

Money for healthcare

The Covid-19 pandemic brought sadness for many people. But there were also moments of joy and gratitude. One man who used his time during lockdown for good was Captain Sir Tom Moore. In the spring of 2020, at the age of 99, he began to walk laps around his garden. He walked to raise money for the UK's National Health Service (NHS). This was his way of thanking the NHS workers who put themselves at risk to save the lives of others. Sir Tom became a national hero and raised more than £30 million for charity.

Preventing hunger

In 1942, during the Second World War, a group in Oxford, UK were saddened by news of starving people in Greece. To help, they campaigned for food supplies to be sent to Greece. This group became known as The Oxford Committee for Famine Relief. After the war, they expanded their work further. The group is still going today and is known as Oxfam. They are a global charity working to build a world without poverty, where all people are treated equally. Oxfam works in about 90 countries and in 2020 helped more than 25 million people living in poverty.

Kind Inventions

Humans are great inventors. Many inventions are created to make life easier or better in some way. Some inventions were born out of kindness, with the spark of creativity coming from seeing someone else in need. Here are just a few incredible inventions that make life easier, safer or healthier for humans, animals or the planet. Maybe they might inspire you to make something that could help others!

Blobs, an invention to help the environment

A company in the UK, called Notpla, has created edible packaging that can hold liquid. It can be used instead of a plastic bottle, with the goal of reducing plastic waste. The ball-shaped edible blob is made from seaweed extract and can be filled with water or other liquids. So far, it has been used during running races and music festivals. But it could be used to get clean water to disaster areas, too.

FrogLog, an invention that's kind to frogs

Swimming pools can be dangerous for small animals such as frogs, lizards, squirrels and mice. If they fall in, they might struggle to climb the steep sides to safety. The FrogLog is an inflatable platform with a ramp that gives these creatures an easy way out of the pool to dry land.

Stair-climbing chair, an invention for wheelchair users

A group of university students from the Swiss Federal Institute of Technology in Zürich, Switzerland, created a cool robot that could climb stairs. Soon after, they saw a new potential for their invention. They added a seat and adapted the robot to become a wheelchair! In 2017, the students founded their company Scewo, and launched a groundbreaking, stair-climbing electric wheelchair.

Polyglu, an invention that gives people clean drinking water

In 2002, a Japanese company invented a special powder made from soya beans. They called it Polyglu. When mixed into dirty water, the powder sticks to the dirt. It then sinks to the bottom of the container, leaving clean water above. After filtering, the water is safe to drink. Polyglu could save lives in very poor or disaster-hit places, where there is no clean running water.

Seabin, an invention to help the oceans

A project called Seabin was developed in Australia. Its goal is to clean up the oceans one piece of litter at a time. Each Seabin sits in a harbour, sucks in water and, with it, rubbish. Volunteers help empty the bin. Then, scientists monitor the waste to find out exactly what items are polluting the water. Each bin collects 1.5 tons of rubbish every year.

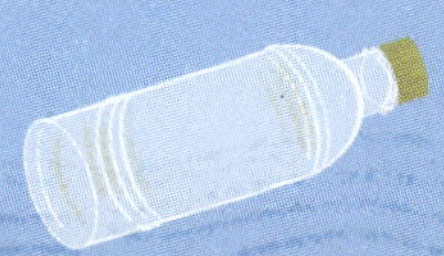

Kindness in War

Ever since humans first lived in groups, there has been fighting and war. War brings cruelty and violence upon innocent people. But there can also be moments of kindness. Both on and away from the battlefield, people help the wounded, protect and rescue civilians and care for orphans. Many brave people find small ways to be kind during wartime.

The Angel of Marye's Heights

Sergeant Richard R. Kirkland served as a soldier in the American Civil War. In 1862, during the Battle of Fredericksburg, he heard cries of agony from fallen soldiers on the battlefield. Unable to ignore them, he climbed over the wall that was protecting him. At first, he was shot at as he gave water to the wounded. But when soldiers from both sides understood his kindness, they cheered! He was nicknamed 'The Angel of Marye's Heights'.

The Red Cross Movement

There was much suffering during the Second Italian War of Independence in 1863. Swiss businessman Henry Dunant was shocked and saddened by this, so he urged world leaders to do more to help victims of war. It also gave him an idea: to train groups of people to provide help during times of war. The project became The International Federation of Red Cross and Red Crescent Societies. It provides protection and help for victims of war and violence all over the world.

Anne Frank's friend

World War II lasted from 1939 to 1945. During this time Germany's Nazi government discriminated against and murdered about 6 million Jewish people. Many Jewish people had to go into hiding. The Frank family hid in the attic of their company building in Amsterdam, Netherlands. Their employee, Hermine 'Miep' Gies, risked her life to secretly bring them food and supplies. Young Anne Frank spent her days in hiding writing her diary. Sadly, the Franks were discovered in 1944, and within months, Anne and her mother and sister were killed. Miep kept Anne's diary, and after the war gave it to Anne's father Otto, who had survived. Otto published Anne's now-famous diary and the world learned of Miep Gies' kindness.

Hero of the Rwandan genocide

In Rwanda there are two different ethnic groups – the Hutus and the Tutsis. In 1994, a conflict between these groups erupted into a brutal civil war. One Hutu woman, Zura Karuhimbi, set out to save as many Tutsi people as she could. She hid them in her small two-room home and surrounding fields. She knew that if the soldiers found out, she might be killed alongside them. Karuhimbi's only weapon against the army was to scare them. She threatened to unleash spirits on them and their families if they harmed her or the people she was hiding. Amazingly, this worked! She may have saved more than 100 people from harm.

Bravery in the Balkans conflict

In the 1990s, the Balkan region of Europe was torn apart by conflict. During this time many Bosnian Muslims were killed by Serbian forces. However, some people disobeyed orders and tried to help those in need. One such person was Pero, a Serbian police officer. He forged papers to allow some of his Bosnian neighbours to escape the country. One of those neighbours was 12-year-old Kenan Trebinčević. Thanks to Pero, he and his family were able to flee to America and start a new life there.

Standing Up for Others

There are times when a person, or group, might need others to speak up on their behalf. This is often because those people are not given a voice within society. One way that people can make themselves heard is through social media. Or they might write stories or songs that can be read or heard. Throughout my life, I have tried to stand up for others and the planet in my own way. First I did this by walking. Now, I do this by speaking to others about how to be kind to the Earth.

Music with power

In 2020, ten-year-old Mila de la Garza from Los Angeles, USA experienced racism from one of her classmates. She and her band The Linda Lindas decided to speak out. The band wrote a song to empower anyone who has been oppressed. They hoped to use their voices for those who weren't able to. Their punk rock song criticized the boy's actions, and it soon went viral. The Linda Lindas used music to get their opinions heard. Now other people who have experienced racist behaviour know that they are not alone.

Beyond the football field

Marcus Rashford is an English professional footballer. In 2020, he used his fame to stand up for something beyond sport. He campaigned for many children in the UK to be given food vouchers in the school holidays as well as during term time. Growing up, his family didn't have much money. This meant that he understood how, for some people, it can be a struggle to put food on the table. Rashford wanted to stand up for these families. He said that 'as long as they don't have a voice, they will have mine.' This started a wider movement. Now, many restaurants offer free meals to children in need, too.

Hip-hop environmentalism

Hip-hop artist Xiuhtezcatl Martinez has been a climate activist since the he was six years old. Martinez's Aztec heritage has shaped his love for the Earth. He belives that being kind to the planet goes hand-in-hand with being kind to people. Martinez is a 3rd generation co-founder of the Earth Guardians. This organization helps politicians understand how climate change affects indigenous communities and the world. Martinez uses his music to spread this message.

Peaceful Protests

Protesting is a way to show that you think something is unjust. For example, my way of protesting the bad treatment of the planet was to stop using oil. There are many different ways of making a stand. Sometimes it helps if other people join in, too. This can make governments take notice, and encourage them to make changes for the better.

Mahatma Gandhi leads the Salt March

Between 1858 and 1947, India was ruled by the British. The Indian people were treated badly. For example, it was illegal for them to produce or sell salt. Salt was important for cooking, but it had to be bought from the British. An Indian lawyer and activist named Mahatma Gandhi decided to protest. On 12 March 1930, Gandhi and a group of his followers set off on a 24-day march. They walked to the sea to collect salt. Lots of people joined and the movement spread around the country. Eventually, India gained freedom from British rule.

The Singing Revolution

For many years Estonia struggled under the rule of other nations. In 1944, it became part of the Soviet Union and this caused many Estonian traditions to die out. One of these traditions was choral singing, so the Estonian people decided to use it as part of a peaceful protest. From 1987 onwards, large crowds of Estonians gathered in public. They joined hands and sang their national songs as an act of defiance. In 1988, 100,000 Estonians spent five nights singing protest songs together. This event helped Estonia finally achieve independence in 1991.

Black Lives Matter

Black people in America suffer racism, violent treatment and sometimes even death at the hands of the police. In 2013, activists Patrisse Cullors, Alicia Garza and Opal Tometi decided they had had enough. They started the Black Lives Matter movement to stand up for Black people's rights to dignity and safety. They aimed to work peacefully with all people in the spirit of kindness and humanity. In 2020, George Floyd was murdered by police officers in Minneapolis, USA. This sparked grief, outrage and protest all over the globe. Millions of people united behind the movement.

Rosa Parks sits tight

In 1955, the American South was segregated. This meant that Black people were badly treated and had to stay apart from white people. For example, Black people had to sit in a special section at the back of buses. Activist Rosa Parks was taking the bus home one day when the bus driver told her to give up her seat for a white passenger. Rosa refused to budge, so she was arrested and put in jail. This helped to spark a big movement with many Black people refusing to use public buses. This support led to the unfair rules eventually being changed.

Women's March

In 2017, around 5 million people protested against discrimination. They took part in marches all around the world to support equality for girls and women. They also marched for LGBTQ+ and civil rights and environmental causes. They were driven by a feeling that discrimination towards women and other groups of people was on the rise. So they joined forces to show that it would not be tolerated.

Standing up for Nature

Nature needs kindness from us just as much as people do. By caring for our environment, we protect the world we live in today. And taking care of our planet today, is a kindness to all living things in the future. Many people around the world have seen that the planet needs help, and have decided to take action. Looking after nature is an extra special type of kindness.

The Green Belt Movement

Wangari Maathai was born in Kenya in 1940. After returning from university, Maathai discovered that the forest near her home was being cut down. The forest provided food and shade for her local community. Unfortunately, hers was just one of many forests being cut down across Kenya. So in 1977, Maathai started the Green Belt Movement. This project encouraged women to plant trees in their local neighbourhoods. The people who wanted to cut down and sell the wood grew very angry with Maathai for standing up against them. She was arrested and beaten for her activism. But thanks to her intelligence, strength, and kindness, the Green Belt Movement succeeded. Communities that are part of the Green Belt Movement have so far planted more than 51 million trees.

Nuclear power? No thanks

Nuclear power was invented in the 1950s, and it greatly changed the fuel industry. Nuclear power produces energy by using heat from a nuclear reaction. Some people think it is good because it doesn't create smoke like fossil fuels do. However, it does create waste that remains dangerous to people and the environment for hundreds of years. In the 1960s and 70s people began protesting against nuclear power. The 'Smiling Sun' logo became the symbol of the movement. It is still used today to show opposition to nuclear power.

School strike for climate

Swedish activist Greta Thunberg was eight years old when she learned about the damage that climate change is having on the planet. It troubled her for many years. When she was 15, Thunberg decided to skip school every Friday to sit outside a Swedish government building. Her protest raised awareness of climate change, and before long thousands of people had joined her. The movement also spread around the world. Thunberg has since travelled the globe by boat to spread her message. She has spoken to world leaders and continues to campaign for a brighter future for all. Go Greta!

Bye Bye Plastic Bag project

In Bali, Indonesia, the Wijsen sisters, Melati and Isabel, were tired of seeing rubbish on their beach. It was a beautiful island, but the beach was littered with plastic bags. The sisters decided to make a change. In 2013, they started a campaign to say 'no' to plastic bags. They took their message to the government. Four years later, the country banned single-use plastic bags and straws and pledged 1 billion dollars to reduce plastic pollution.

Everyday Acts of Kindness

Everyone has the ability to be kind. For many people it is something that they do everyday without even noticing! Here are a few examples of everyday acts of kindness. These are small things that people have done just to make others happy. By doing kind acts such as these, we can all help to spread kindness around the world.

Day of kindness

Mister Rogers' Neighborhood was a TV show that ran from 1968 until 2001. The host, Fred Rogers, taught children about feelings, friendship, kindness and acceptance. In 2019, Rogers' home state of Pennsylvania, USA, launched an annual day of kindness. This was to encourage people to share their good deeds in memory of Mr Rogers, who passed away in 2003.

Operation Beautiful

One day in 2008, American writer Caitlin Boyle was having a bad day. She decided to do something kind for someone else in order to cheer herself up. So she began writing anonymous messages on sticky notes and leaving them in public places. Her messages said things like, 'You are beautiful' and 'You are so loved'. Her project turned into a campaign called Operation Beautiful, and many other people joined in. Thousands of inspiring notes have been posted around the world, helping people to feel better about themselves.

Walls of kindness

In 2015 in Iran, a new tradition called 'walls of kindness' began. These walls appeared first in cities, then spread across the country. The walls have rows of pegs for people to hang up and leave any clothes that they no longer want. People in need can then take the clothes for themselves. This is especially useful for people experiencing homelessness during the cold winter, when they might not have anything warm to wear. Some walls also have spaces for shoes and books.

Do Something For Nothing

Every day in London, hairdresser Joshua Coombes saw many people who were experiencing homelessness. He decided to do something to help. So he offered them haircuts. By using his skills, Coombes helped people feel good about themselves. This also allowed him to build connections with people who are often isolated. He started the #dosomethingfornothing initiative, to encourage other people to get involved around the world. He was even joined by a vet who cared for homeless people's dogs.

Suspended coffee

A 'suspended coffee' is when someone pays for a cup of coffee (or food or other drink) in a cafe in advance, for someone else. The idea is that the shop holds the extra money so that they can use it to help someone else later on. It might go to someone who can't afford to pay, or to someone who needs cheering up. It is an anonymous act of kindness to a stranger. The buyer can walk away knowing that they have done something to brighten up another person's day.

Kindness Close to Home

Taking Care of Yourself

Throughout this book we have read many heart-warming stories of people being kind to others. However, we should also remember to be kind to ourselves, too. Taking care of yourself is the first step to having a kinder outlook on life. After all, how can we have compassion for others if we're not healthy and happy? Here are a few ways to slow down and look after number one – that's you!

Listen to your body

One easy way to be kind to ourselves is to tune in to how our bodies are feeling. Are you feeling hungry or thirsty? Tired or bursting with energy? What do you need to make your body happy? Perhaps it's a snack, a nap or a trip to the park. Take notice of what your brain needs to relax, too. You might feel like cosying up on the sofa with a book or watching a film. Doing what makes you feel good is a great way to look after yourself. Just be sure not to hurt or upset yourself or anyone else in the process!

Cut yourself some slack

You are only human. That means you might not get things right all the time. Remind yourself that this is totally okay – no one is perfect. All we can do is try our best. Humans are flexible and can learn from the past. So, if you ever do something hurtful or thoughtless, don't worry! Just remember to apologize, and mean it! Forgive yourself and learn how to do better next time. Making mistakes is how we learn.

Mindfulness moments

The world is a very busy place. We can all benefit from slowing down from time to time. Finding a moment to stop and notice things and feelings is called mindfulness. It can have many positive effects. It makes us more aware of ourselves and others. It even makes us more compassionate. One way to practise mindfulness is to decide to take notice of everyday things. For example, focus on the food that you eat or the sound of birds outside. Another might be to try something new. Try sitting in a different chair as you eat your dinner. This can help you see the world from a whole new angle – literally!

Good Vibes

Many of the people in this book live by the golden rule: they treat others as they themselves would want to be treated. They care about the feelings of others and are compassionate. Being compassionate isn't only about the way that we act. It's also about the way that we think. From the kid next door to history's most famous people, we can all remind ourselves to think kind thoughts about others. Even when we don't want to!

Saying sorry

Can you think of a time when you did something hurtful or unkind to someone else? If not, great! But if you can, that's okay – we all have bad days. The important thing is how we deal with these moments when we realize that we have done something wrong. Remember that an apology can go a long way. Making mistakes is just how we learn and grow. We can't change what we said or did in the past. But we do have control over what we say and do in the future.

Show forgiveness

One of my favourite stories of forgiveness is that of Nelson Mandela. He was the former president of South Africa. In 1964, Mandela was sentenced to life in prison for opposing apartheid. This was a system of segregation and discrimination against Black people in South Africa. Mandela was a peaceful man, and while he was in jail, he treated his jailers with respect. By the time Mandela was released 27 years later, he and some of his jailers had become friends. Mandela forgave his jailers for mistreating him. His kindness even encouraged some of them to change their views about segregation. Mandela's story shows that good can come from forgiveness. Staying angry and holding a grudge will often just lead to unhappiness.

One Act a Day

Do you feel ready to do some good? Why not try doing one kind thing every day? Pay attention to how this affects you and the people around you. Practice makes perfect, so the more kind things you do, the easier it will be. Once you are switched on to the idea of being kind, you might start to notice more opportunities to practise it. Here are a few suggestions to get you started.

Starting small

Aesop is thought to be the author of many famous Greek fables. One in particular is about a lion who spares a mouse's life. Later, the mouse saves the lion's life in return by freeing it from a trap. The moral of the story is that no act of kindness is ever wasted. This advice is still true today. Your one kind act a day can be as simple as smiling at someone you don't know or sharing a treat with a friend.

Paying a compliment

How do you feel when you get a compliment? It feels good, right? Telling someone what you like or appreciate about them is a great way to make others feel good, too. You could even write them a note or a letter to tell them how great they are.

Being thankful

Do you have parents, teachers or other adults who look after you day in, day out? If you do, how about taking a moment to notice all the different things that they do for you? Then say thank you! Is there an act of kindness that you could do for them in return? Try to do something that doesn't create more work for them. For example, if you decide to make them a card or gift, tidy up after yourself. Kind words and a hug can often mean a lot, too.

A Future of Kindness

I'm not sure I could have survived my journey through life without kindness. And if I had managed to survive without it, life would have been pretty grim! When I think about the future and what part kindness will play in it, I start by examining the present. Then, I glance back to the past, as we've done in this book.

My hope for the future is that kindness is used to combat violence and anger. I hope it can help people and nature live together in harmony. People will always have different beliefs, but kindness can be the glue that binds us and heals the hurts that have divided us.

I hope that you have enjoyed the stories in this book, and that they have inspired you to see kindness in your everyday life. While kindness is a part of who we are, I also think being kind is something we have to practise, because being kind is a choice. I hope that kindness will be a part of who we are until the end of time.

So, what is the future of kindness?

The future of kindness is up to you.

Quotes of Kindness

Everyone has the ability to be kind to each other and the planet. But sometimes we might need a little nudge in the right direction. A few words of wisdom can inspire compassion in all of us and remind us that being kind is easy! Here are some wise words to get you thinking.

'It's nice to be important, but it's more important to be nice.'
Dwayne 'The Rock' Johnson, wrestler and actor

'The really fantastic thing about kindness is that it's free!'
Lady Gaga, singer, songwriter and actress

'Compassion and service to others enhances the humanity of all, including that of oneself.'
Desmond Tutu, religious leader and anti-apartheid activist

'Prepare yourself so that you can be a rainbow in someone else's cloud.'
Maya Angelou, poet and civil rights activist

'One love, one heart, let's get together and feel alright.'
Bob Marley, singer and songwriter

'If you see someone without a smile, give 'em yours!' Dolly Parton, country music star, actress and businesswoman
'Be kind whenever possible. It is always possible.' The 14th Dalai Lama, spiritual leader
'Learning to stand in somebody else's shoes, to see through their eyes, that's how peace begins.' Barack Obama, former US President
'Carry out a random act of kindness, with no expectation of reward, safe in the knowledge that one day someone might do the same for you.' Diana, Princess of Wales
'...the love you receive from people around you can become the power that allows you to love yourself, too.' J-Hope, singer and member of K-pop band, BTS

Glossary

activism
The practice of taking action or campaigning to bring about change.

altruistic
When someone is unselfish or shows a selfless concern for others.

ancestors
People from the past from whom a person or a group of people descended.

anonymous
Someone who is not named.

apartheid
A former South African system of racial discrimination. Apartheid did not give people of colour the same rights as white people. Black and other people of colour were forced to live separately from white people.

archaeologist
A scientist who studies past human life. They search for and examine ancient bones and other items to learn about the past.

boycott
To refuse to do something as a way of protesting it.

campaign
A course of action that is organized to achieve a certain goal.

civil rights
The rights that people have to freedom and to be treated as equals.

civilian
A person who is not in the military, police or fire service.

compassion
Concern for others.

dedicate
To strongly support or be loyal to a person or cause.

dignity
A way of behaving that shows you have a sense of pride.

discriminate
To treat certain groups of people in an unjust way.

empathy
The ability to understand the feelings of other people or creatures.

endangered
At risk of becoming extinct.

environmentalism
Concern for and action that is aimed at protecting the environment.

equality
When all groups of people are treated as equal to one another and have the same rights and opportunities.

ethnic
Relating to a group of people who share customs, traditions or religion.

fable
A short story that aims to teach a lesson.

famine
A situation in which people do not have enough food to eat and in which some people die as a result.

filter
To pass a substance through a device in order to remove unwanted substances.

forge
To falsely make or copy something that is not yours. A forgery is used to deceive others, for example a forgery of someone's signature.

fossil fuel
A type of fuel that has formed in the Earth. Natural gas, coal and oil are fossil fuels.

generosity
The quality of being kind, and giving to others.

genocide
When a targeted group of people are deliberately killed.

harbour
An area of sea that is near the coast where ships and boats can moor and shelter.

heritage
The beliefs and traditions that are part of the history of a particular group of people.

hieroglyphics
A writing system that uses pictures to represent sounds or entire words.

hormones
Chemicals in the body that regulate processes within the body – for example how the body grows or develops.

immune system
The parts of the body that are designed to fight diseases and infections. The immune system includes cells, tissues and organs.

Incan Empire
An area that spanned from northern Ecuador to central Chile and was controlled by the Inca people from around the early 1400s until the 1530s.

indigenous
Relating to the earliest known inhabitants of a place.

intrepid
Adventurous or fearless.

moral
A lesson that is taught by a story.

oppressed
When someone receives harsh treatment from a government or other institution.

orphan
Someone who doesn't have any living parents.

outlawed
When something has been banned or made illegal.

pandemic
An occurrence of a dangerous disease that affects lots of people at the same time.

pledge
A promise or agreement.

poverty
The state of not having enough money to survive.

proverb
A short saying that states a belief or truth, or gives advice.

racism
The bad treatment of a person or group of people because of their race.

respect
To admire someone.

segregation
The practice or policy of keeping people of different races or religions separate from one another.

social
When someone is happy spending time with others.

sponsor
To pledge to give someone or a group of people money.

Taoism
An ancient Chinese philosophy. Taoism is based on the writings of the Chinese philosopher Laozi.

tuition
Money that is paid to a school or university in order to study there.

vaccine
A drug given to people or animals to help protect them from a certain disease.

Index

Selected Sources

'A Country Created Through Music', The Atlantic (www.theatlantic.com/international/archive/2015/11/estonia-music-singing-revolution/415464)

'An Interview with Bernhard Winter, Forbes (Europe 2019) Science & Healthcare', Medium (www.medium.com/the-logician/an-interview-with-bernhard-winter-forbes-europe-2019-science-healthcare-369082e419f9)

Anne Frank House (www.annefrank.org/en)

Black Lives Matter (www.blacklivesmatter.com)

Bregman, Rutger ***Humankind: A Hopeful History*** (Bloomsbury Publishing, 2020)

Bye Bye Plastic Bags (www.byebyeplasticbags.org)

Captain Tom (www.captaintom.org)

Do Something For Nothing (www.dosomethingfornothing.org)

'Double Tigers', World Wildlife Fund (www.worldwildlife.org/initiatives/double-tiger)

Educate Girls (www.educategirls.ngo/Home.aspx)

'Finding the Man Who Saved My Family', Slate (https://slate.com/news-and-politics/2014/04/kenan-trebincevic-finds-the-man-who-saved-his-family-20-years-after-the-balkan-war.html)

Fridays for Future (www.fridaysforfuture.org)

Malala Fund (www.malala.org)

Nomads Clinic (www.upaya.org/social-action/nomads-clinic)

Notpla (www.notpla.com)

'Obituary: Rwanda's Zura Karuhimbi, who saved dozens from genocide', BBC (https://www.bbc.co.uk/news/world-africa-46618482)

Onondaga Nation (www.onondaganation.org)

'Operation Beautiful', Healthy Tipping Point (www.healthytippingpoint.com/ob)

Planetwalk (www.planetwalk.org)

Seabin (www.seabinproject.com)

Thunberg, Greta 'The disarming case to act right now on climate change' TEDxStockholm, November 2018 (www.ted.com/talks/greta_thunberg_the_disarming_case_to_act_right_now_on_climate_change?language=en)

Titanic Belfast (www.titanicbelfast.com/history-of-titanic)

Trinkaus, E. and Villotte, S. 'External auditory exostoses and hearing loss in the Shanidar 1 Neandertal'. PLoS ONE, 2017 (www.doi.org/10.1371/journal.pone.0186684)

Women's March (www.womensmarch.com)